EAST OF SORROW

Marc Hudson

Grateful acknowledgment is due to the editors of the following
magazines in which the poems below first appeared:
Arts Indiana: "Morning Rounds"
The Cape Rock: "My Alluvial Reveries"
Christianity and Literature: "Composition in Yellow"
Fine Madness: "Helen's Tears"
Kestrel: "Ecce Homo" and "If Walt Whitman Is Grass"
the new renaissance: "The Sandstone Meditations"
O Tempora: "Above the Gunnison"
Poet Lore: "Final Bath" and "My God Once Gazed at Me"
The Silk Road Review: "The Sugar Creek Sutras"
"Composition in Yellow" originally appeared in *Christianity and
Literature*. Reprinted with   permission.
"Letter to Miranda" was first published in *The Sewanee Review*,
vol. 119, no. 3, Summer 2011.

ISBN 978-0-9973102-4-5

Printed in the United States of America

RED MOUNTAIN PRESS

Santa Fe, New Mexico

www.redmountainpress.us

In memory of my teachers and mentors in the craft

Nelson Bentley

John Haines

Leslie Norris

ACKNOWLEDGMENTS

I am grateful to Wabash College for sabbatical support during the time some of these poems were written. Thanks are also due to Jody Bolz, editor of *Poet Lore*, for her helpful criticism, and to Susan Gardner, editor and publisher of Red Mountain Books, for her imagination, criticism, and support. I owe special thanks to George Core, editor of *The Sewanee Review* for forty-four years, and my editor for thirty of those years. His generous support and critique of my writing was a gift I cannot repay.

With unending gratitude, I thank my family: Our son, Ian, now gone, for his courage and his abiding genial spirit that compelled me to write some of these poems. Our daughter, Alix, for her big-hearted young life as a bilingual especial education teacher and playwright and company member of Teatro Paraguas in Santa Fe. I draw strength from your shimmering energy. My beloved Helen, I thank you for your belief in my poetry and in me, for all the good dinners and conversations, your tough-minded optimism, and your faith that life is ultimately good.

I

A WORD TO MY READERS

A poem has been deleted,
and a forty-page lacuna follows,
my nekyia, my night sea journey,
the crossing of the wept waters
after our Ian died. I have spared you
the interminable poem of ten thousand drafts.

In lieu of all those dreadful terza rimas,
the tedium of a stranger's grief,
I will indulge myself this much—

Always, I am swimming the waters of Acheron
following the frog kick of our son,
    down and down
past where our lives are driven.

There, I've had my say.
Be grateful: turn the page.

READING OF CLASSICAL CHINA

I ask my students
to write in the manner
of Tu Fu.

I look out the window
at the last of summer
taking its leave,

imagine
the cold rain
striking the cut sunflowers,

the tussock
where the earth humps up,
as yet unsettled.

I think I will go
and sit in the rain
until I become rain.

He Hears the Hyla and Thinks of Orpheus

They sing into evening,
monks in chapels
of skunk cabbages:
beget, beget, beget

and continue all night
in a powder-green rain
reeking of silage and ruminating
beasts.
          Rain and frogsong
fill the night,
the Eros-swollen membrane.

Orpheus, they say,
was dismembered by maenads,
his harp set among the stars.
He is here in the frog echolalia:
Hyla regilla,
Rana aurora aurora.

Eurydice stands
by a cobra-hooded
swamp flower.
She likes the song so well
she has forgotten
she is dead. The frogs
gaze forward.
In a tenor not meant for her,
they sing.

THE PLAINT OF NATURE

for Wendell Berry

At dusk it was I spoke to her,
Dame Natura, under the hydrangeas
brimming with flies, one warm evening
in late July. I was on my knees
weeding the garden and there she was
stroking a leaf. I must have started
for she smiled then and spoke reassuringly
in the old Latin. She wondered why
I was seeking her. When I could find
my tongue, I said a friend had asked
about her and so I'd set about
tracing her footsteps among the medievals.

"Strange," she replied, "that one you speak of
visits me each Sabbath in his woodlands.
His haunts and mine oft coincide."

"True, Lady, but it grieves him
our recent poets have had so little to say
about you."

"Not so long ago, there was one," she remembered.
"He was going blind writing pamphlets
for the Puritans, so I let him glimpse
my ankle. Such a bookish lad!"

A goldfinch twittered at her elbow
and another worried the stubborn seed
of a sunflower. I kept squinting—
at times her face was still as one
carved in marble, and at times
you could read a planet's grief on her brow.

"Tell your friend," she said at last,
"I won't be absent long from their verses.
Poets cannot forget what is theirs to speak."

She fell silent, and I saw in her gaze
the vanishing glaciers, shorebirds scattered
from their nesting places—the continual
erasure of species. I wanted to ask her
whom Alain had called the Vicar of God
what is the poet's work in such a world,
but her sorrow gave me pause. And the moment
passed. It was as if a prism had fallen
into the grass directing the sun
to where she had stood, but now the light
shone elsewhere. Nonetheless,
I lifted my hands as one does
when the Cup is given.

ELEGY FOR AN OLD POEM

On the Poem Itself

Call it a tideland: you learn mortality there.
An oar blade sprouting acorn barnacles,
the mandible of a shield crab,
all debris of the trivial dead,
their stench and shine, amount to the same thing.
The vellum is smudged and blotched as a carapace,
beer-stained by drunken scribes,
a ledger soaked in human salt and the sea's.

The Audience

To them, Heorot was a song, something heard
between the roaring of wind in the fir
and the harp at smokefall. The scop sang on—
they saw a gracious woman
pouring mead. Those tapestries were brief
as ember walls of a sinking fire
or a singer's breath.

Shield Sheaving

Grain-god, giver of the branch,
he comes from the sea penniless.
They call him gannet boy, swan prince,
bastard of the fallow waves. It's as if the sea
brought forth wheat. At his death, they stand
by the shore, empty-handed gleaners.

THE LAST SURVIVOR

Late-comer, he had not seen
the falcon risen from the king's fist,
the hushed floating through smoke and rafter.
Only from hearsay did he know
how light resurged when the harper
braided the bright water, leaf and branch
on the naked ridge. Even the famous scabbard
a rotten husk of iron. He could not drag
the metal back, the garnets no longer gripped
by cloisonné, were like hard eyes that will not shut
even in death. He must second-guess a world
from rusted pins and harness buckles,
recover the crescent moon from the dark
cavity where a skull has lain.

My God Once Gazed at Me

My God once gazed at me
through my son's eyes when I seated him on the toilet
and when I dressed him in his green Nike shirt
and denim shorts and when I placed his feet
in his orthotics and strapped them on like greaves.

Now I see my God in the grass and in the ants
living and dying among those blades
and in the blue shards of church glass,
St. John wrapped in the tongues of fire.

Mornings and evenings, I carried the burden
to which I prayed. Sometimes my God would smile
when I lifted him from bed
or when I knelt before his wheelchair
fastening his feet to the foot plates.

ECCE HOMO

It is Christ in the tomb I wish to consider, Christ
unrisen, with the bloody wounds in his side,
as Thomas saw them—his beautiful face
inscrutable in its stillness, Christ
in his naked sex and broken hands—
not the risen god who harrowed hell,
made death his trophy and sits on his throne,
King Harry after Agincourt—
no jubilant emperor this one,
but a young man lying still and forsaken,
like the first word in the book of winter.

FINAL BATH

Only Saturday, when I squeezed the last
of the coconut shampoo into my palm,
& lathered your hair, you laughed,
leaning forward on your straps. Water
streaming down your chin made a brief
translucent beard.

This morning, I borrow
a hospital's wash cloth, dip it in a basin,
& daub your face, the fuzz along the line of your jaw,
your narrow chin. With great care, I trace
the rigid wing of your left arm, while your mother
stands opposite, performing the same silent office.

Saturday's ablutions were under the sign of *Top Hat*,
Fred & Ginger swirling in the mist, "dancing
cheek-to-cheek again" amid scarlet arpeggios, while we
listened to Casey Kasem's Top Forty—me clucking
at the insipid love lyrics to a surfer boy, you cracking
up at my antics, mocking my aged tastes
with a sidelong squint. I loosened your chest straps &
laved your shoulder blades, a little brusquely perhaps,
surprised again you were no longer a boy,
but a lithe young man with a swimmer's shoulders & lats,
narrow hips and, how shall I put it,
your virginal male beauty?

Now I pass the cloth over your chest,
your skin strangely flushed where the blood has pooled
above your heart. (Or is it from the EMT's
frantic lunge at your stillness?)
Now down the relaxed slats of your belly,
along your thighs, marbled calves, lovely
ungainly feet, our cloths sweep
as if, together, we are Christ
ministering to the desert body of Christ.

Under their long lashes, Ian, your eyes appear
half open. Most carefully, they seem to be considering
a difficult equation. Has your breath contrived
somehow to continue without its body,
the way a boat does, when its oars are shipped
and it lifts into the further wave?

A Figure of Christ as the First Element

Around Him silence,
the roaring of snowmelt in late May,
time of the feast of Corpus Christi.
Snail-slime rivulets glisten in the coal-dark
seams of the glacier. Soon water will gush again,
meal-grey with powdered rock.

Christ is silent under the knotted scourge
of Herod's slaughtermen,
the Cross on Him trestle-heavy
as a cliff of breccia. Yet, over it all,
the harp-light of falling water flashes.

Longinus lifts the spear,
stoneblind under the rock face of the riven
Christ. Water breaks from the glacier,
cuts and scours the plates of basalt.
He takes the wound, and the cirque wall,
each spidery crevice, is lettered with fire.
Son of Man, come kneel and drink.
That which suffers death is also this.

HELEN'S TEARS
March 2003

We lay him down, we let him go,
his mother, his sister, and I,
into the wooden hull of his coffin
with its brass fittings, into the furrows
of the winter earth. We say good-bye.

Since then, no thaw:
Only sleet and wind and the mustering
of an army. Our son, like one of those gone
for a soldier to the Gulf, one of the myriad
terra cotta minions buried with the Emperor,
Ian Geoffrey Hudson, 19. Now the blind ones
pin a shroud over *Guernica* and parley of war,
now they posture, "Operation Shock and Awe."
Hot metal will rain on Baghdad. A human dust
will rise and mingle with the red Tigris wind,
dust as fine as the snow that blows over Indiana today
will gather in clouds and refract the sunlight
over Benares. Countless particles will ride the jet streams
east over the Pacific, providing nuclei for rain to fall
on Olympic forests, into sword ferns and salal,
the cataracts of the Elwha and the Hoh,
and some few, perhaps, will soldier on over
the Continental Divide, to drift down as droplets
into Iowa or Illinois or maybe as far as this watershed
of the Wabash, of Rock River, to fall like Helen's tears
after the burning of Ilium, the death of Priam and his sons
dispersed into the world the molecules of sorrow
but falling that day as individual crystals of snow
on my son's grave, making what is so unbearable
appear beautiful. Friend, fellow citizen,
war is the worst inhuman thing.
And burying your child, even in peace,
is like placing into a boat every little possession
you held dear, and pushing it into the breakers.

II

MORNING ROUNDS

When I step out at seven with Alix in my arms,
the sun is a red disk
barely clearing the houses down the street,
mists are curling up from front lawns.
We go slowly, the two of us,
hearing the muffled voices from inside,
husbands murmuring over coffee,
a young father calling, "Good-bye, Christian,
good-bye," as he starts up his car.
Why do these ordinary sounds please me so?
Is it they proclaim somehow we're safe,
we've grown up out of the darkness
like seedlings shouldering aside the heavy cairns
of the grains of soil, alive in a well-tended moment?
That we're here with the fuchsias dangling
from the baskets and the swan-necked planters
coiling with ivy? Is that it?
Still, I'm watchful of the shattered,
root-humped pavement under the big trees
and of my newborn, who, eyes shut,
is buzzing to herself a low contented sound.
I want her to fall asleep, but not too soon.
And before I reach the corner, she opens her eyes,
she stares straight up through the maple crowns.
Not tree, nor leaf, nor even green she thinks,
but simply light and not-light swirling into
each other, alluring, forever nameless.
She smiles and I float above her face
gazing exactly down into those eyes
which cannot focus yet
and so are zenith blue
and vague as cloud. Suddenly,
I realize, if I could leave my skin
like a sheath, she might see
more clearly who I am.

Because the milkweed pods
have begun to split,
our daughter helps them along.
She opens them up and scatters the down,
singing to each wisp of seed,
"Go on your way, little sister,
wherever you want to."

The shoulder and sleeves of her dark jumper
are white with them,
the ground of our garden
is snowed under.

To those seeds I would say,
 "Fly over the darkening year,
the sleet that turns to slanting rain
in our warming atmosphere. Wait
for an April when we are gone.
Monarchs depend on you. We all do."

Composition in Yellow

Against the coming darkness, the sunflower lifts its many
blazing crowns & the monarch tumbles into the milkweed
burdened with eggs. I saw this as I came from the garden
with three red zinnias and a sprig of yarrow
for my son's grave. There is yellow enough here
what with the Coreopsis & the butterweed & the pollen
baskets & dusty abdomens of bees, the cucumbers
clambering up the stout stems of the sunflowers,
the daisies & the daylilies & the squash blossoming
out of the green chaos of the compost.
Ah, the profuse swelter of July, his birthday month,
my Leo son's, the cowlick of his yellow hair remembered
in the innumerable rays & coronas of the Compositae.

For the Players of Teatro Paraguas and
Word Over All

Sainted Day, Santo Domingo, Señoras y Señores,
this morning on Vuelta Place in Santa Fe—
because last evening we saw our daughter
become a hawk fledged with poetry,
as just a moment before she'd been a distant listener,
enumerating the names—bobolink, tanager,
white-crowned sparrow—of birds passing
in the watches of the night. She among nine others
became Dionysus, the deathless
music of eels in black water, of dallying eagles
and barbaric yawps—they sounded the depths of Walt,
they lifted us to the alturas of Neruda, then plunged
us back into the dying body of a boy, a father's kiss
on his forehead. We were lifted even as we fell
by those dancers on the half-lit stage, those debtors
to language. The guitar, it throbbed and moaned
like a phantom limb, it sutured the wound
in the body of the world. And the voices, always
the voices, and the words, always the words
made flesh, the vowels with their multihued wings,
the difficult consonants blocked like us by lips
and tongues and teeth, hatreds, hungers, and love—
upon that stage those players suffered for us,
Sainted Day, and so we live.

Letter to Miranda

Milano 1621

for Alix

Dear Miranda, my wonder, how is it
Ten years have passed? You sit on Naples' throne
And I, again, pretend to rule Milan.
You have children of your own, older than
You were when we came to our island. Does
It call you back? The wind in the shore grass,
The chatter of fulmars on the far cliffs,
Those first few precious days when Caliban
Was not our slave?
                              I walk in my worn cloak
Down from the Castello, pass the vendors
Hawking crosses and charms in the plaza.
I can't slip by the matrons. They give me
The Evil Eye, thinking I still possess
My magic. Some few dare approach, begging
Respite from their chilblains. Like wetted straw
The ancient syllables cannot catch fire.
I want art to enchant. The other day,
In the Duomo, I was pestered
By a priest: "Why come when you don't believe?"
I stared the cretin down. "To pray," I said.
How can one, my dear wonder, not believe
When there are such isles as ours?
                                          Our small boat
Broke up in the wild surf. I found your hand
And managed to get us to the tidemark,
Where I sprawled, retching. I could somehow sense
You standing there, unafraid, the water
Like bracelets round your ankles. When I had
Collected our few trunks and laid my books
To dry among the matted kelp, I wept
Our wreckage. You wandered down the wide beach
Stooping here and there, tilting your head
To listen. Next you lifted to my lips
A shell. "Drink, Father," you said. "Fresh water."
Daughter, I stopped weeping and gazed at you
In wonder: your small hands, the shell's rough spines,

Your solemn eyes, regarding me with pity.
(I keep that gaze in a velvet place.) We
Found a dry cave and tinder for a fire.
The eggs of murres, rockfish and black mussels—
That was our first supper. I salvaged some
Sun-warped boards for your bed. And there I tucked
You in, unattended but for the gulls
On the far rocks. You asked for a story.
"Once upon a time and on an island lived
A wizard and his daughter. Prospero
His name was. Guess her name, Miranda. It
Means wonder."
                    I never told you the dream
I dreamt that night. Your mother came to me
And sang through the doors of the sea. She sang
As if she stood in her garden, the waves
Like waist-high flowers, the constellations
Like clematis trained to a crumbling wall.
I rose and came to her. Her song became
The vellum she gave me, whose Latin words
Swirled into claws and beaks and flaming wings
Which lifted from each leaf—Daemons that linked
Like vertebrae of one great Serpent curved
Into itself, sinuous tail in mouth, burning
And turning, faster and faster, until
I read each writhing word or sang it
Rather, music of the animate Earth,
In the chain-mail of the Snake, the mouth
Of my love pressed against mine. This magic
Didn't come from Cornelius Agrippa
Or thrice-great Hermes. It was the island's,
The open folio of the Ocean
I read that night, each footfall of the wind
Over the bay, each mist-shape and cape
Concealing as they came into being
My wizard's robes, seaweeds where Proteus
Never slept. Pines where eagles roosted, shells,
Caves, moon-illumined coracles, I
Traced the small labyrinths inside each cell.
I learned the secret names of things. At dawn
I fell into exhausted sleep. I woke
On another shore, island no more. That day,
Wandering the island, we found new springs

Fringed by anemones, colonies
Of murres and gannet clouds, and that
Timid boy, Caliban. I do not say
It was an idyll. We had so little.

Dukes make poor carpenters: our chairs all wobbled
And cups slid from our table. Elementals
Know nothing about rulers. Atomies
Move in circles. Still the shy boy showed us
Brine pits, the barren places and the fertile,
Oyster shoals, fulmar eggs: all his wealth he
Shared, that feral boy whom we taught letters.
He leaped across the tideland rocks, quick-footed
As his mind was nimble. On the tablet
Of the beach, you wrote your first painful words.
Soon M and A shimmered through surf.
Among the maze of islets, I read you
Homer's thundering hexameters: Sounds
You loved but letters left you cold. "Father,"
You asked, wrinkling your brow, "Why are words so
Still and the world so quick?" "Breath, Miranda,
Brings them to life. Put them in your mouth and
They stir. Words can remember when the hand
That wrote is dust."
                    But Caliban taught you
Better. Against the wingbeats of so many
Birds, the four strong winds and the spilling waves
Europe never stood a chance. You had speech
I never learned, a Creole all your own.
And while the island studied us, I delved
Into Proclus and nursed my revenge. I
Hadn't forgot Antonio's evil.
I took the dream the island gave to me,
Mated it with my deepest hate. A growth
Took root inside my brain. I kept seeing
Antonio's eyes as his men grabbed me
And thrust me in the boat. They were remote
And cold. My brother whom I trusted watched
Approvingly. Hate is a force like fire,
An igneous cancer. It takes deep root,
If you let it.
              With my first charm, I tore
Open some rotten tufa. Split a fir

Tree with my second. Then, remembering
Milan, the sweet pears in my garden, dropped
A cliff into the sea. I laughed, my cackling
Echo reverberating in the cave.
Then watching sea-birds wheeling, understood
My lethal magic: how could I explain
To you what I had done? Coming to my senses,
Remembering you, I clambered up the island's
Hogback spine: at the summit, lightning-struck,
Twisted by wind, stood a huge pine. I heard
Strange moaning, I dismissed at first as wind
Rocking the tree. Then something silver stirred
In the humped dirt—a girl's face, glint of mica—
A wing. In that root-cage was Ariel
Penned by Sycorax, dwindled to insect.
With a humming, slow cadence, I unhinged
The tree, lifted the tiny mewling thing
From the tangle of roots. For warmth, I placed
It in my shirt. It nuzzled there as at
My breast. When you returned with Caliban,
You took her in your hands and fairly danced.
So elementary school had begun.
You named the nameless one, Ariel. Me
She did obey, but you she loved.

Twenty years and more it's been. Caliban
Is back among his people. Ariel
Belongs to the wind, you to your kingdom.
What father's words have I for one so young
And wise? The island raised you, lifted you
In beauty. Sometimes myth is truer than
Science, and love trumps hate. I see your face
Among the glancing waters of my fountains,
Your voice the exact translation of light
When it first was spoken. "O brave new world,
That has such people in it!" So you lifted
Your eyes from the chess board, you saw them all
With love's true gaze—Alonso, Gonzalo,
And Sebastian, dear Uncle Antonio.
You know them now for what they are, and me
As well. Naples, they say, is a chaos
Of narrow streets that grottoes undermine,
A theater of pickpockets and cunning.

Any city beneath Vesuvius
Is only ruled by day. But Ferdinand
Is good, if dull. I saw his eyes, saw how
He gazed at you and was comforted. Power
Is ever a problem. Look round the world!
Arrogant fools hold sway. I rule with fewer
Illusions. This I know: distrust, ignore
Any intelligence that whispers war.
Keep your kingdom small or do not keep it
At all. Yet I trust your good heart, Miranda,
The clear wellsprings you drank from as a girl.
I write you and so correspond with all
The creatures. You learned them by their true names
Not ours. The planet is not ours. You help
Me keep this knowledge. Keep teaching this creature.
I see you gazing over the wide bay
At the Isles of Ischia, hipbones
Of Parthenope. May they remind you
Of what you knew, wandering the island
Those years ago. Visit, when you can, those
Far shores. I wish I had some swift white bird
To send you a song at your casement window—
Of the island's magic, I have these letters.

With all my love,
Your father, Prospero

LATE SUMMER STANZAS

1

Goldfinches, balancing
on the backs
of sunflowers,
prying loose
the large, dark seeds,
cracking them
open to get the meat.

September pays good wages
when beaks are strong
and seedheads many.
They build the house
of late summer, goldfinches singing,
hammering long into the evening.

2

Picking basil leaves,
kneeling under purple-
tipped spikes,
inhaling a Tuscan
pungence.
          The oils
seep into my fingers,
and the bees compete with abandon.

I gather fistfuls of the fragrance—
and still I have the upper hand,
the promise of bruschetta.

3

These white butterflies,
their three prominent purple
spots and leaf-hued
underwings—they hover,
grazing the long sprigs.

          And the furred bumblebees
who have fattened all summer
have taken possession
of my basil. They buzz
indignantly, then return
to their drowsy supper.

Fair enough—
we can all share
the largesse of basil.

4

And I came and saw
under the sunflowers

whole cities of
gold-bodied bees,

the last of a busy race
singing from their slender cupolas,
gathering in their green basilicas

and the bright traffic of those streets
streaming with winged
commerce, instantaneous
systems of transport!

A Garden in Western Indiana

What do they do in the darkness,
the hollyhocks and Helianthus?
About this hour, photosynthesis
shuts down, the nightshift takes over,
and I walk for awhile in the garden.

The fennel injects a little anise
into the air, and I imbibe
its green liqueur. Whatever was siphoned
from the atmosphere, drips back
in a different vein. I drift

over the floor of an ocean,
and the dead put their oars
into the conversation. Juan de la Cruz,
tell me, why did you go barefoot
on the road from Fontiveros?
And, Walt Whitman, that inchworm
I saw this morning, hauling a grain
of pollen in its mandibles, why
did I think of you and your measureless poem?

The basil is starting to bolt, I reach down
and pinch its blossoms. Begging your pardon,
codling moth. And you, my mammoth
sunflower with your tattered wooly
crown, I will stake you soon.

So my foolish thoughts run in the darkness
and the din from those workshops
is like the beating of waves
on Cape Perpetua. The fennel's
a filter-feeder sieving the air
above the crinoid beds of Sugar Creek.
Sculpin drift among the fronds
of my kale. A seahorse has come to port
in the Sargassum of my cucumbers. And there
is the Kraken further down in the benthos
where I wrestle America each night.

More and more, I wade the distance
between the living and the dead.
To the north, my son seeks my gaze
from his stony hill above the high school.
South is the Super Walmart, its phosphorescence
an algae bloom on Lethe's wharf.
East is Granada: my daughter dreaming
the fountains and towering elms
of the Alhambra.

              Now the first bird,
a thrush I think, enters the poem.
A bat scribbles through the air. Beyond
the still-sleeping houses, the trumpet-shaped
silhouette of the tornado siren, the morning star
burns, uneclipsed. For a moment,
my perplexity rests.

              Then I remember the sea,
how near it seems even here, the moon flowers
of this night garden under the foam
of Queen Anne's Lace. It beats upon our headlands,
unceasing as the wind across its smoking crests.

I bow my head between the living and the dead.

If Walt Whitman Is Grass

then William Stafford is lichen
subsisting on boulders above the timberline,
a pioneer symbiont
at the cold edge of possibility.
And if Robert Frost
might be seen as eastern hemlock,
then Stafford is the neighborly organism
pointing the traveler north.

I never saw him
precisely as a man, even in person
could never bring that plain,
unassuming face into focus.
So I liken him to this reticent
habitué of granite.

Once, after hearing him read,
I walked out into Seattle rain
feeling a strange elation,
as if I were the acolyte
of a mild-mannered apocalypse,
as if through infinite space
a fine mist were processing,
blurring well-kept boundaries.

So I imagine him dissolving
the speeches of politicians
the way lichen softens, then
assimilates, the most obdurate rock.

MY ALLUVIAL REVERIES

I would like to lie down among the loess hills of western
Iowa and stretch and yawn as I haven't since I was seven.

I would lie there a long while and listen to the wind
beating on the soft anvils of grass

and perhaps a goldfinch would light on a thistle
and take possession with his twittering song.

Out over the Missouri all afternoon,
cumulus would be building. I would relax more deeply

into the land, my shinbones brushing up against
the Flint Hills of Kansas, that country

where clouds outnumber the cattle.
Nor would I scant Nebraska in the drift

of my sentiments, my atoms trending toward
the shallows of the Platte, the mud of her

meandering channels and catfish islands
off toward Ogallala. I would bide my dissolution

a long while, even as the contrary wind
would be sifting me

back with the grains finer than loess,
the pollens and spores and swirling rotifers,

east unto my wife's country, the farm in Grand Meadow,
the cottonwoods that ensconce the Little Sioux.

A Cabin at Hood Canal

White-footed mice
have invaded my house.
They nibble my soap
and patter across the stove
to the pan of burnt potatoes—
a slight sound,
but enough to get me thinking.

So much goes hungry
this time of year. I thought
a sack of rice and an oyster
bed would see me through winter,
but her shelves are stocked
with corn of the coldest.

So the mice and I
keep house together
while hunger troubles our sleep.
It gnaws on our dreams,
and drifts with the cormorant
where the moon shows her ribs.

THE HOUSE AT ARLES

He hummed all afternoon
under his wide-brimmed hat.
He made a solarium
where goldfinches
for Eternity might feed—
yellow and then
more yellow—
in friendly competition
with the flare of first light.

Dusk those days
was slow to come
and he reluctant
to leave the garden.

At a table under the trellis,
we sat down.
I filled our beakers
with the dark Chianti.

And so we drank
deep into the evening.

III

THE SANDSTONE MEDITATIONS

for Arden Skoog

1

Water drips

over feathery moss,
fractals of fern,
glittering—

frets, channels
friable stone,
scours out basins,
fills them—

under the dark overhang,
a green light,
a quickening
like an ovum pierced by sperm.

Then flows on,
the good daughter
going home,
a whiteness gliding

down through cedar,
intricate shadow—
the obedient creature
of whose beauty

we are the scar.

2

Years ago at Hood Canal—

a boy plucks from the mud
the domed shell of a moonsnail,

brings his mother
that horn dripping darkness.

Gravely, she receives the trophy
and smiles down at him,

innocent of how much heavier
in her hands than his

is this gift that weighs them.

3

This wall of Upper Mississippian
Sandstone, this outcropping
of the old ocean
(whom the Saxons
called "Spearman,"
but I would always name
"wife," "woman")—
this tidal wave of rock
slowly breaking
whose fossil pockets of algae
have weathered out,
leaving a honeycomb, a
marrowbone,
vertiginous with time.

How easily a man may fall
from this cedar-fingered rim
down the escarpment
as doves scatter and his life-
skein spools out
on random thumbs of rock—

but it's just as easy to fall
standing here, bolt upright
on terra firma, transfixed
by that watery old wall,
that Paleozoic shell,
its knobs and sockets

the apparatus
of an absent intelligence.
And turned inward on itself
like those mortuary statues—
those korai of ancient Crete—
adolescent girls
for whom death came
more quickly than a boy.

4

There are many doorways here,
a clamor of small voices
sounding through porous stone.

And leaves are sailing
scarlet and gold
where the creek divides
at Canoe Island.

Each day the sycamores
drift in deeper pools.

5

On this yielding stone
blurred sometimes beyond deciphering
are cut the names
of lovers and solitary men—
Fraser, Haines, and Bolton—
married to their eroding dates.

And two great dove-like birds,
their bodies stippled with intricate care,
recede into the stone, year by year.
And here's a bas-relief
of Satan himself—his nose
flattened like a veteran pugilist's
and eyes sunken as if
gazing back to the garden he lost

for good. (Though he maintains
a villainous leer and sprouts
a manly horn.) Hands
of the artisans all but flutter
about the stone, wingbeats
of those birds hurtling toward
extinction.

And I wonder: is the matrix
by definition always woman,
while these inscriptions—
sensual, ineffectual—
are masculine? Must men
mark time with their long
shadows, while overhead,
higher than our hopes,
the Magna Mater breaks
and breaks our hearts?

6

Though Arden is gone from the shore,
her son plays horn for an island band,
bright swatches of jazz, blues
like "Melancholy Baby." His fingers
flash on the brass valves, he blows
a riff like a ring of light. He holds
the bronze note. And were there gods,
they'd listen with delight, as if
a garden were assembling in the air
for their symposia.

So on pleasure cruises around Orcas,
the retired accountant
who pays good money,
the surgeon from Mukilteo
whose one request is always
"Moon River," like his style.

And it still can amaze him,
those nights he plays
the sentimental numbers

and the couples sway out on the floor
unsteady after their gin and tonics,
the wash of waves under foot,

and Lummi Island off in the fog
like a sail-bladed reptile
and the cormorants with their cork-screw necks,
the starfish clustered on their ledges—
how they swirl together in the drink,
the drunken, protean selves.

And suddenly he's blowing on the moonsnail,
lip to lip with darkness.
He's helpless as a girl
at the onset of menarche—

he becomes, for a moment,
that final thing—
a man cognate to flowing water.

A Few Songs from the Sixth Extinction

I remember the demented trillings
in the rain-washed Willapas west of Skamakowa,
the *gick gick* of cricket frogs, insomniac
nights Northern Virginia 1955,
and not so long ago, the *tonk tonk*
from a small pond near the derelict
Dari King on the road to Shades, Indiana—
as if a drunken monk
were pounding on a rain barrel.

Who among us can remember Viosca's Frog,
its whistle of an Ivorybill
from old growth Louisiana bottomlands?
Or the pippids of Surinam, the plantannas
of Central Africa warbling
under the cold tarns of volcanic mountains.

And in el Valle de Antón,
in the ancient crater there, the small creek
called "The Thousand Frog Stream"—
you had to step most gingerly
on the green bank, so many golden ones
had gathered. Who can speak of their music
without falling silent?

And the Giant Tree Frog, its song of a rope
jerked through an unoiled pulley, its creaking
of a mechanism in need of repair.

Their silence is the silence of dead water.

Ear Over Eye

1

In this clear light
and this light wind
much is given,
hidden or unheard—

A tree swallow skims
an insect from the stream

and a vulture spirals down
to collect a parcel
left by the road.

Light decides
what can be seen.

2

A thrush is singing
from its covert in the pines.
Clear, ethereal, three
or four phrases, each
its own pitch.

The ear delivers
each syllable to its audition.

THE SUGAR CREEK SUTRAS

1

Swallows dip and swerve
under dark overhangs

and water drips
from those green walls,

slips down the tip of a fern,
as over the bronze

of a temple bell.

2

This stone is an escritoire
not unlike Mother's
rolltop desk. It conceals
small drawers
for the storage of ideas.
It has a ledge for writing
utensils and a lamp
of great wattage some distance
above.

Often, of a late spring afternoon
someone is writing there
where the creek cools
her bare instep.

3

A wren calls
with a voice so like water
water might do well
to learn her song.

Diminuendo is her domain.

4

Translucence—
the condition of first leaf—

light
intersecting a lattice

that is all
but nothing—

from this, depends
a planet.

5

Those dry bronze
leaf covers of the beech tree
sprinkle the forest floor.

And the litter from the tulip
poplar—orange-striped
bits of saffron.

Meanwhile, in the canopy,
a silver maple
completes its mosaic.

6

Autumn will flower in its own way—

less and still less,
the concision of what is.

ABOVE THE GUNNISON

We climbed in a grey wind,
you, my barefoot daughter,
contemplative like me,
pausing now and then
to study the workers
toiling by an ant-hill
or the glitter of a far cliff
emerging from cloud.

We climbed steadily
toward a radio tower
with its array of microwave antennae,
wind-warped chain link fence,
and signs warning
of dangerous frequencies
as in another age
pilgrims might have climbed
to a wayside temple
and a sacred pool.

We said little,
sharing the ample stillness
of a mountain afternoon.
An ease crept between us,
we who often find words
too difficult.

And so we paused, drinking in
the wide green valley of the Gunnison,
the muted silver of the river
and the shadows of the mountains
beyond the clouds. Their shoulders
held in the light, unseen,
I felt, palpable enduring rock.

As we started down, we heard
far thunder, and then
a volley of nighthawks
swept over us, crying fiercely.
I said, "They are fleeing

the storm." "No," you spoke
in gentle correction.
"They've come to hunt
in the early darkness."

Down the mountain
we made our slow
descent, me occasionally
stumbling on loose stones,
you, more sure-footed behind me,
careful of the small
toilers underfoot, collecting seed
at the end of summer.

INTO THE HEART OF THE ANDES

*"All my life I have imagined that of all mortals I was the one
who had risen highest in the world—I mean on the slopes of
Chimborazo."* —Alexander von Humboldt

Three stratovolcanoes on my kitchen table—
topo maps, that is, of Volcán Cayambe,
"Source of All Waters," Cotopaxi,
"the Neck of the Moon," its nested
craters and almost perfect cone, and that summit,
Chimborazo, most distant from Earth's center,
I will climb. I'm dusting off my Danner boots
then pulling my pack from the attic, fitting
every zippered niche of it with matches and flint,
field glasses, fishing line and limestone sinkers.
And, how could I forget? My compass
and Peruvian wool cap, the crampons and ice axe
with which I ascended Snæfellsjökull
thirty years ago. Plus a hand lens for studying lichen
and von Humboldt's *Kosmos* (much abridged).
I've submitted to the Dean a request
for an indefinite extension of my sabbatical:
I'm going it alone into the depths
of "The Heart Of the Andes," that great canvas
by Frederic Edwin Church, presently hanging at the Met.

You raise an eyebrow, as if to ask, "At your age?"
Humboldt was no younger on his final expedition.
Old men should be explorers and I am ready now.
There is a footpath climbing with the mildest of gradients
into the left foreground—the one by the half dead tree
hung with epiphytes, on whose blasted trunk the artist
has inscribed his name and the year, 1859.
A little further on, a native boy in a blue serape
kneels by a wooden cross, beside him, his brother,
reverently gazing down. I will ask them, "¿Quién
está enterrado aquí?" Did he die in the cataract so near
it chills them with its spray? I'll say an Ave there,
remembered from my Jesuit days at Georgetown,
and tell the local saints, especially Our Lady
of the Hydrologic Cycles, I will behave myself.

I plan to camp by that waterfall and become acquainted
with her inscapes, her braided tresses and blowing
mists, the sound and form of water enveloping flora.
Ekphrasis is contemplation, and thunder resembles
the silence of prayer.

But now a caracara in the shadowy bosque is calling.
It is dark with intimations of *The Origin of Species*,
the spiraling, incessant mutations of DNA.
Across the waterfall, a pendant bush
bears blue calyces, the very flower Novalis knew.

It may be months before I reappear
famished, having virtually subsisted on herbs and roots—
then look for me by that doorway
to the colonial church, in the slumbering lakeside village
of adobe dwellings. There I'll spend my hundred years
of solitude, a chrysalis dreaming and waking
in its long siesta, hatching plans:
from the beginning, it has always been thee, Chimborazo,
where glaciers and lava make a perfect weld
and ice sublimates into cloud, I will conquer.

On the high llano, I'll pitch my tent, gather brush,
build a small fire—that smudge right there—
and brew a pot of yerba mate. Lifting my cup,
I'll watch the mountain and wait for the moon to rise.
Come dawn, I'll lighten my pack and wade
the milky stream. My eyes peeled for paving
stones of porphyry, I'll pick up the old Inca road
and cross the lofty **Páramo** of Azuay. Then follow
a condor to the heights of Chimborazo—

tomorrow. This evening, though, it is still early
May, 1859. The vast canvas in its carved wooden frame
is lit by gas light. The last, reluctant guests
are being ushered from the hall. And Humboldt,
in Berlin, is also taking his leave, the great naturalist,
from his planet. Turn down the lamp,
draw the heavy curtains. Gabrielle
has just closed her uncle's eyes.

ALONG THE WILDCAT

for John Tritt

1

Draped in scales
dark bronze and black

is this specimen
Nerodia sipedon.

Asleep on a branch,
half-submerged,

it seems to be listening.
I lift my oar more quietly.

2

That full moon at Sixbey Camp
a flashlight swept over the creek.

Swirling in that cone
came a host of mayflies,

their mortality softly
overlapping our own.

3

And there was that one
sycamore leaning far out over the creek,

its bare roots an intricate weave
among rounded stones.

It held the shore intact
by instinct or enchantment.

4

All morning long
canoeing in the rain

water enters water
in a constant welling.

Which way is it going
in this rising that is also

a falling, in this
small and endless

death that is our life?

Reading the *Sefer Tehillim*, Shades State Park

That October afternoon
I had in my satchel
a little red wine, some Merlot,
and that small book of free translations,
Stephen Mitchell's *Book of Praises.*

I poured some wine on the forest
floor, and lifted the slender
book and read—"Blessed
are the man and the woman. . . "

The wine had a dark
undertaste or maybe it was the light
falling through the falling
leaves of my last sabbatical,
but the psalms in paraphrase
rang true.

I saw how the leaves
needed only a little nudge
to detach themselves and become
bronze or golden boats
adrift in the currents of air.

And I read on, illumined
and lifting my glass
to the leaves and the late hatching
ephemerae. I will confess
more times perhaps than necessary
I toasted those leaves
and the dying insects
in the gold smoke of their one
and only day. I drank
to the Order Diptera
and to the gisms of that winged pair
who had found each other
among the words of the First Psalm.

I dare say it was holy
and blessed were they
though only a kind of fly.

And it was not unbecoming
to drink to them
and to lift in praise
my little cup of language
in this falling world.

THERE IS AN ANCIENT LIGHT

that falls across the adobe wall
and the ladder leaning there.
It takes most seriously
the back rest of the wrought iron chair,
the slender arch of its shadow.

Thanks to this light,
the evening is at anchor
and whatever shape
that cloud assumes
that is the shape
I place here on this page